Confidence

Unlock Your Inner Potential and Transform Your Life with Proven Strategies and Expert Insights: The Ultimate Guide to Building Unshakeable Confidence and Overcoming Limiting Beliefs in All Areas of Your Life, from Career to Relationships and Beyond - A Must-Read Self-Help Masterclass!

Lance P. Richards

Confidence: Unlock Your Inner Potential and Transform Your Life with Proven Strategies and Expert Insights: The Ultimate Guide to Building Unshakeable Confidence and Overcoming Limiting Beliefs in All Areas of Your Life, from Career to Relationships and Beyond - A Must-Read Self-Help Masterclass!

Copyright © 2023 - All rights reserved. No part of this book may be reproduced in any form or by any means without permission in writing from the publisher, LPR Publishing. Please read the full disclaimer at the end of this book.

Table of Contents

01: Introduction: The Importance of Confidence

Confidence is a powerful force that can transform your life in countless ways. When you have confidence, you are more likely to take risks, pursue your goals, and achieve success. You are better equipped to handle challenges and setbacks, and you are more likely to bounce back from failure. You are more resilient, more adaptable, and more capable of overcoming obstacles.

At the same time, confidence is not always easy to come by. Many of us struggle with self-doubt, negative self-talk, and limiting beliefs that hold us back. We may worry about what others think of us, or we may feel like we are not good enough. We may struggle to assert ourselves, to speak up, or to take action.

Fortunately, confidence is a skill that can be learned and developed over time. With the right strategies and insights, you can unlock your inner potential and build unshakeable confidence in all areas of your life.

In this book, you will learn proven strategies and expert insights for building confidence and overcoming limiting beliefs. You will discover the power of positive self-talk and affirmations, and you will learn how to identify and challenge your inner critic. You will gain an understanding of fear and how it impacts your confidence, and you will learn mindset shifts for turning negative thoughts into positive ones.

You will also learn the role of self-care in building confidence, as well as the connection between confidence and success. You will discover the benefits of confidence in personal and professional relationships, and you will learn communication skills, body language, and non-verbal communication.

You will gain insights into public speaking and networking, as well as navigating imposter syndrome and building confidence in the workplace. You will learn how to deal with rejection and failure, and how to handle feedback and constructive criticism.

Additionally, you will learn how confidence impacts decision making, leadership, and social situations, as well as dating and relationships. You will learn about the importance of boundaries, raising confident children, and the connection between confidence and health and wellness.

01: INTRODUCTION: THE IMPORTANCE OF CONFIDENCE

Furthermore, you will gain insights into mindfulness and meditation, gratitude, creativity, and overcoming perfectionism and procrastination. You will learn about the role of self-compassion in building confidence, as well as tips and techniques for building resilience and overcoming burnout.

By the end of this book, you will have a comprehensive understanding of the importance of confidence in all areas of your life, and you will have the tools and strategies you need to build unshakeable confidence and transform your life. You will be equipped to overcome limiting beliefs, negative self-talk, and self-doubt, and you will be able to take action with clarity, conviction, and confidence. This book is a must-read self-help masterclass for anyone who wants to unlock their inner potential and achieve success in all areas of their life.

02: Understanding Confidence: What It Is and What It Isn't

Confidence is a term that is often used in many contexts, from personal development to business and leadership. It is often referred to as a quality that successful people possess, and it is something that we all aspire to have. However, it is not always clear what confidence really means or what it entails. In this chapter, we will explore the concept of confidence, what it is, and what it isn't.

First, it is important to understand that confidence is not the same as arrogance or conceit. Arrogance is an overbearing sense of self-importance, while conceit is excessive pride in one's own achievements. These traits are often accompanied by a sense of entitlement and a lack of consideration for others. Confidence, on the other hand, is a belief in oneself and one's abilities that is tempered by humility and a sense of perspective. Confident people are aware of their strengths and weaknesses, and they are able to balance their self-assuredness with a healthy dose of self-awareness.

Confidence is also not the same as extroversion or gregariousness. While extroverted people may seem more confident on the surface, introverted people can be just as confident, if not more so. Confidence is not about being the life of the party or the center of attention. Rather, it is about being comfortable in one's own skin and being able to express oneself authentically, regardless of the situation.

Confidence is also not something that is innate or fixed. While some people may seem to be born with a natural sense of confidence, it is a quality that can be developed and cultivated over time. It is not something that you either have or you don't have. Rather, it is a skill that can be learned, practiced, and improved upon.

So, what is confidence, then? At its core, confidence is a belief in oneself and one's abilities. It is the ability to trust in one's own judgment and decision-making skills. It is the willingness to take risks and try new things, even in the face of uncertainty or potential failure. It is the ability to bounce back from setbacks and learn from mistakes. It is the capacity to handle challenges and obstacles with grace and resilience.

Confidence is also closely tied to self-esteem, which is the sense of worth and value that we place on ourselves. When we have high self-esteem, we are more likely to feel confident in ourselves and our abilities. Conversely, when our self-esteem is low, we may struggle with self-doubt and negative self-talk, which can undermine our confidence.

It is also important to note that confidence is not a one-size-fits-all quality. What makes one person feel confident may not have the same effect on another person. For some, confidence may come from their appearance or physical abilities. For others, it may come from their intellectual or emotional intelligence. Ultimately, confidence is a subjective experience that is unique to each individual.

In summary, confidence is a belief in oneself and one's abilities that is tempered by humility and self-awareness. It is not the same as arrogance or extroversion, nor is it an innate or fixed quality. Rather, it is a skill that can be learned, practiced, and improved upon. Understanding what confidence is and what it isn't is a crucial first step in building unshakeable confidence in all areas of your life.

03: The Power of Positive Self-Talk and Affirmations

The way we talk to ourselves has a profound impact on our confidence and self-esteem. Positive self-talk and affirmations are powerful tools that can help us build a strong sense of self-belief and overcome limiting beliefs that hold us back from reaching our full potential. In this chapter, we will explore the power of positive self-talk and affirmations, and how they can transform your life.

Positive self-talk is the practice of consciously changing the way we think and talk to ourselves, from negative and critical to positive and encouraging. Our internal dialogue has a direct impact on our emotions, behaviors, and actions. When we engage in negative self-talk, we create a self-fulfilling prophecy that reinforces our limiting beliefs and undermines our confidence. On the other hand, when we engage in positive self-talk, we empower ourselves with the belief that we can achieve our goals and overcome obstacles.

Affirmations are a form of positive self-talk that involves repeating positive statements to oneself, usually in the present tense. Affirmations can be used to focus on a specific goal or to cultivate a general sense of positivity and self-belief. For example, an affirmation for confidence might be, "I am confident in my abilities and trust in my decisions."

Research has shown that positive self-talk and affirmations can have a significant impact on our mental health and well-being. They can reduce stress and anxiety, improve our mood, and increase our overall sense of self-worth. Positive self-talk and affirmations can also help us overcome self-doubt and negative thought patterns that hold us back from pursuing our dreams and goals.

To effectively use positive self-talk and affirmations, it is important to be mindful of our thoughts and feelings. Pay attention to the words and phrases you use when talking to yourself. Are they negative and critical, or positive and encouraging? When you catch yourself engaging in negative self-talk, try to reframe your thoughts in a positive and constructive way.

When using affirmations, choose statements that resonate with you and that align with your goals and values. Repeat your affirmations daily, either silently to yourself or out loud. Visualize yourself achieving your goals and embodying the qualities you want to cultivate. Consistency and repetition are key when it comes to affirmations, so make them a regular part of your routine.

It is also important to recognize that positive self-talk and affirmations are not a magic bullet that will instantly transform your life. Building confidence and self-belief takes time and effort. Positive self-talk and affirmations are just one tool in your arsenal, alongside other strategies such as setting goals, taking action, and seeking support from others.

In conclusion, positive self-talk and affirmations are powerful tools that can help us build unshakeable confidence and overcome limiting beliefs. By consciously changing the way we think and talk to ourselves, we can cultivate a strong sense of self-belief that empowers us to pursue our goals and dreams. Remember, the way you talk to yourself matters - so make sure it's positive and uplifting.

04: Overcoming Limiting Beliefs: Identifying and Challenging Your Inner Critic

Limiting beliefs are the negative and self-defeating thoughts that hold us back from achieving our goals and living our best lives. They are the voices of our inner critic, the part of our mind that tells us we are not good enough, smart enough, or capable enough to succeed. Limiting beliefs can manifest in all areas of our lives, from our careers to our relationships and personal growth.

Identifying and challenging limiting beliefs is essential for building confidence and achieving our goals. In this chapter, we will explore the common types of limiting beliefs, the impact they have on our lives, and strategies for overcoming them.

Common Types of Limiting Beliefs

Limiting beliefs can take many forms and can be deeply ingrained in our subconscious minds. Some of the most common types of limiting beliefs include:

– "I'm not smart enough"

04: OVERCOMING LIMITING BELIEFS: IDENTIFYING AND CHALLENGING YOUR INNER CRITIC

– "I'm not talented enough"

– "I don't have enough experience"

– "I'm not attractive enough"

– "I don't deserve to be happy/successful/loved"

These beliefs are often based on negative experiences or messages we received in childhood, but they can also be reinforced by societal expectations and cultural norms.

The Impact of Limiting Beliefs

Limiting beliefs can have a profound impact on our lives, both personally and professionally. They can lead to feelings of self-doubt, anxiety, and low self-esteem. They can also prevent us from taking risks, pursuing our dreams, and reaching our full potential.

For example, if you believe you are not smart enough to pursue a particular career, you may avoid applying for jobs in that field or shy away from opportunities to learn and grow. This can limit your career options and prevent you from reaching your full potential.

04: OVERCOMING LIMITING BELIEFS: IDENTIFYING AND CHALLENGING YOUR INNER CRITIC

Strategies for Overcoming Limiting Beliefs

Overcoming limiting beliefs requires a conscious effort to identify and challenge them. Here are some strategies that can help:

– Identify Your Limiting Beliefs: Start by becoming aware of the negative thoughts and beliefs that hold you back. Write them down and examine them objectively. Ask yourself where these beliefs came from and whether they are true or not.

– Challenge Your Beliefs: Once you have identified your limiting beliefs, challenge them. Look for evidence that contradicts them and ask yourself whether they are helping or hindering you.

– Reframe Your Thoughts: Replace negative self-talk with positive affirmations and reframed thoughts. For example, if you catch yourself thinking "I'm not good enough," reframe that thought to "I am capable and worthy of success."

– Take Action: Challenge your limiting beliefs by taking action. Do something that scares you or pushes you out of your comfort zone. This can help build confidence and challenge negative self-talk.

– Seek Support: Talk to friends, family, or a therapist about your limiting beliefs. Getting support and feedback from others can help you gain perspective and overcome negative thought patterns.

In conclusion, overcoming limiting beliefs is essential for building confidence and achieving our goals. By identifying and challenging our inner critic, we can break free from self-defeating thought patterns and cultivate a strong sense of self-belief. Remember, you are capable of achieving anything you set your mind to, so don't let limiting beliefs hold you back.

05: Understanding Fear and How It Impacts Your Confidence

Fear is a natural human emotion that has evolved to help us survive in dangerous situations. However, when fear becomes irrational or excessive, it can have a significant impact on our confidence and ability to live our lives to the fullest. In this chapter, we will explore the nature of fear, how it impacts our confidence, and strategies for overcoming it.

The Nature of Fear

Fear is a complex emotion that is triggered by a perceived threat. It is a natural response that activates the fight, flight, or freeze response in the body, preparing us to respond to the danger at hand. While fear can be helpful in some situations, such as when we need to quickly avoid physical harm, it can also be a hindrance when it becomes excessive or irrational.

The Impact of Fear on Confidence

When fear becomes excessive or irrational, it can have a significant impact on our confidence. It can prevent us from taking risks, pursuing our goals, and living our lives to the fullest. Fear can manifest in many ways, including social anxiety, performance anxiety, and phobias.

For example, if you have a fear of public speaking, you may avoid opportunities to speak in front of others, even if it could benefit your career or personal growth. This can limit your opportunities and prevent you from reaching your full potential.

Strategies for Overcoming Fear

Overcoming fear requires a conscious effort to identify and challenge it. Here are some strategies that can help:

– Identify Your Fear: Start by becoming aware of the fears that hold you back. Write them down and examine them objectively. Ask yourself where these fears came from and whether they are true or not.

– Challenge Your Fear: Once you have identified your fear, challenge it. Look for evidence that contradicts it and ask yourself whether it is helping or hindering you.

– Reframe Your Thoughts: Replace negative self-talk with

positive affirmations and reframed thoughts. For example, if you catch yourself thinking "I can't do this," reframe that thought to "I am capable of handling this challenge."

– Face Your Fear: Challenge your fear by facing it. Take small steps to confront your fear, such as speaking in front of a small group before speaking in front of a larger audience. Gradually increase the challenge as you become more comfortable.

– Seek Support: Talk to friends, family, or a therapist about your fear. Getting support and feedback from others can help you gain perspective and overcome negative thought patterns.

In conclusion, fear can have a significant impact on our confidence and ability to live our lives to the fullest. By identifying and challenging our fears, we can break free from self-defeating thought patterns and cultivate a strong sense of self-belief. Remember, you are capable of overcoming any fear that stands in your way, so don't let it hold you back from achieving your goals and living your best life.

06: Mindset Shifts: Turning Negative Thoughts into Positive Ones

Our thoughts are powerful tools that can greatly impact our confidence and overall well-being. Negative thoughts and beliefs can hold us back from achieving our goals, while positive thoughts can help us overcome obstacles and reach new heights. In this chapter, we will explore the power of mindset shifts and strategies for turning negative thoughts into positive ones.

Understanding Negative Thoughts

Negative thoughts can take many forms, such as self-doubt, criticism, and self-blame. They can be triggered by past experiences, beliefs, and the environment around us. Negative thoughts can impact our confidence by creating a cycle of self-defeating behavior. For example, if you believe you are not good enough, you may avoid taking risks or pursuing opportunities that could lead to personal growth.

The Power of Positive Thinking

Positive thinking involves intentionally focusing on positive thoughts and beliefs, which can help cultivate a more optimistic outlook on life. Positive thinking has been shown to have numerous benefits, including increased confidence, improved relationships, and better physical health.

Here are some strategies for turning negative thoughts into positive ones:

– Identify Negative Thoughts: Start by becoming aware of negative thoughts when they arise. Write them down and examine them objectively. Ask yourself whether they are true or not.

– Reframe Negative Thoughts: Once you have identified negative thoughts, reframe them into positive ones. For example, if you catch yourself thinking "I can't do this," reframe that thought to "I am capable of handling this challenge."

– Practice Gratitude: Practicing gratitude can help shift your focus from negative thoughts to positive ones. Start by writing down three things you are grateful for each day, no matter how small they may seem.

– Use Positive Affirmations: Positive affirmations are

powerful statements that can help shift your mindset towards positivity. Create affirmations that resonate with you
and repeat them daily.

– Surround Yourself with Positive Influences: Surrounding
yourself with positive influences, such as supportive friends,
mentors, or positive media, can help reinforce positive
thinking and beliefs.

– Practice Mindfulness: Mindfulness involves being present
in the moment and observing your thoughts without judgment. This can help you become more aware of negative
thought patterns and learn to let them go.

In conclusion, mindset shifts are a powerful tool for cultivating confidence and positivity in all areas of your life. By
identifying and reframing negative thoughts, practicing
gratitude and mindfulness, and surrounding yourself with
positive influences, you can shift your mindset towards positivity and achieve your goals with confidence. Remember,
your thoughts have the power to shape your reality, so
choose positive ones that empower and uplift you.

07: Gratitude and Self-Reflection: The Key to Building Confidence

Gratitude and self-reflection are two powerful tools for building confidence. By cultivating a sense of gratitude, you can focus on the positive aspects of your life and start to shift your mindset from one of scarcity to one of abundance. By engaging in self-reflection, you can gain a deeper understanding of your thoughts, feelings, and actions, and begin to make positive changes that will help you build the confidence you need to achieve your goals.

One of the most important benefits of gratitude is that it helps you focus on the present moment. When you're grateful for what you have, you're less likely to worry about what you don't have. This can help you feel more content with your life and less anxious about the future. In addition, studies have shown that people who practice gratitude on a regular basis are happier and more satisfied with their lives.

To cultivate gratitude, try keeping a gratitude journal. Every day, write down three things you're grateful for. These can be big things like your health or your relationships, or small things like a beautiful sunset or a delicious meal. By focusing on the positive aspects of your life, you'll start to train your brain to look for the good in every situation.

Self-reflection is another important tool for building confidence. By examining your thoughts, feelings, and actions, you can gain a deeper understanding of yourself and the world around you. This can help you identify the limiting beliefs and negative thought patterns that are holding you back, and begin to make positive changes.

One way to engage in self-reflection is to journal. Write down your thoughts and feelings, and reflect on the events of your day. You might also want to try meditation, which can help you quiet your mind and gain a deeper understanding of your thoughts and emotions.

In addition to gratitude and self-reflection, it's important to take action to build your confidence. This might mean setting goals for yourself, practicing self-care, and challenging yourself to step out of your comfort zone. Remember that building confidence is a process, and it's important to be patient with yourself as you work to overcome your limiting beliefs and develop a positive mindset.

As you begin to build your confidence, it's also important to surround yourself with positive influences. Seek out people who support and encourage you, and avoid those who bring you down. You might also want to seek out a mentor or coach who can help you stay on track and provide guidance and support as you work towards your goals.

In conclusion, gratitude and self-reflection are powerful tools for building confidence. By cultivating a sense of gratitude and engaging in self-reflection, you can gain a deeper understanding of yourself and the world around you, and begin to make positive changes that will help you achieve your goals. Remember that building confidence is a process, and it's important to be patient with yourself as you work towards your goals. With time and effort, you can unlock your inner potential and transform your life with the power of confidence.

08: The Role of Self-Care in Building Confidence

Self-care is a crucial component in building and maintaining confidence. It involves taking care of one's physical, mental, and emotional well-being to enhance one's sense of self-worth and positivity. The idea of self-care can be broad and varied, ranging from simple actions such as taking a hot bath or going for a walk to more intentional practices like meditation or therapy. In this chapter, we will explore the different ways in which self-care can help to boost confidence and how to incorporate it into your daily routine.

Self-care can help to reduce stress and anxiety, which are two major factors that can negatively impact confidence levels. When we take care of our physical health by exercising regularly, getting enough sleep, and eating a balanced diet, we are better equipped to manage stress and anxiety. This, in turn, can lead to a more positive mindset, increased self-esteem, and greater overall confidence.

Mental and emotional self-care are also important in building confidence. It involves taking care of our mental and emotional health by setting boundaries, saying no to commitments that do not align with our values, and practicing self-compassion. When we engage in practices such as journaling or therapy, we can gain greater self-awareness and insight into our thoughts and emotions, leading to more positive and empowered perspectives.

Incorporating self-care into our daily routine can seem daunting, but it doesn't have to be. It can be as simple as taking a few minutes each day to practice mindfulness or gratitude. Starting small and gradually building up to more intentional self-care practices can be a helpful way to make it a sustainable habit. It is also important to remember that self-care looks different for everyone, so finding what works best for you is key.

When we prioritize self-care, we are sending a message to ourselves that we value our well-being and that we are worthy of taking the time to care for ourselves. This can lead to a positive cycle of self-love and confidence-building. Additionally, practicing self-care can help us to develop a greater sense of self-awareness and self-compassion, which are key elements in building confidence.

In summary, self-care plays a crucial role in building and maintaining confidence. It involves taking care of our phys-

08: THE ROLE OF SELF-CARE IN BUILDING CONFID-ENCE

ical, mental, and emotional well-being and can help to reduce stress and anxiety, increase self-awareness and self-compassion, and lead to a more positive mindset. By incorporating self-care into our daily routine, we can enhance our sense of self-worth and ultimately build unshakeable confidence.

09: The Connection Between Confidence and Success

Introduction

Confidence and success are inextricably linked. Whether you want to excel in your career, build fulfilling relationships, or pursue personal goals, having confidence is essential. The reason why confidence is so important is that it is the foundation of all achievement. When you believe in yourself, you are more likely to take risks, overcome obstacles, and persevere in the face of adversity. Conversely, when you lack confidence, you are more likely to hold yourself back, avoid challenges, and settle for less than you deserve. In this chapter, we will explore the connection between confidence and success and show you how to develop the confidence you need to achieve your goals.

The Relationship Between Confidence and Success

Confidence and success go hand in hand. People who are confident tend to be more successful in all areas of their lives than those who lack confidence. This is because confidence gives you the strength and determination to pursue your goals, take risks, and overcome challenges. When you

are confident, you are more likely to try new things, step out
of your comfort zone, and push yourself to new heights.
This is why confident people are often more successful in
their careers, relationships, and personal lives.

One of the key benefits of confidence is that it helps you to
develop a positive mindset. When you are confident, you
believe in yourself and your abilities. This means that you
are less likely to be affected by setbacks and failures, as you
see them as opportunities for growth and learning. You are
also more likely to have a positive outlook on life, which can
help you to attract success and opportunities.

In contrast, people who lack confidence often have a negative mindset. They may be afraid to take risks or try new
things, and may be quick to give up in the face of challenges.
They may also be more prone to negative self-talk and self-
doubt, which can further erode their confidence and self-esteem.

Developing Confidence for Success

If you want to be successful in life, it's essential to develop
your confidence. Here are some strategies you can use to

build your confidence and achieve your goals:

– Identify your strengths: Take some time to reflect on your strengths and talents. What are you good at? What do others admire about you? By focusing on your strengths, you can build your confidence and believe in yourself.

– Set goals: Set clear, achievable goals for yourself. When you achieve your goals, you will feel a sense of accomplishment and pride, which can boost your confidence.

– Practice self-care: Taking care of yourself physically, emotionally, and mentally can help you to feel more confident and capable. This can include getting enough sleep, eating a healthy diet, exercising regularly, and practicing relaxation techniques like meditation.

– Surround yourself with positive people: Spend time with people who support and encourage you. Avoid negative people who bring you down or undermine your confidence.

– Practice visualization: Visualize yourself achieving your goals and feeling confident and successful. This can help you to develop a positive mindset and build your confidence.

– Take action: Take small steps towards your goals every day. When you take action, you build momentum and start to see progress, which can increase your confidence and motivation.

Conclusion

Confidence is the key to success in all areas of your life. By developing your confidence, you can build a positive mind-set, overcome challenges, and achieve your goals. Remember that confidence is not something you are born with, but rather something you can develop over time. By using the strategies outlined in this chapter, you can build your confidence and unlock your inner potential.

10: The Benefits of Confidence in Personal and Professional Relationships

Confidence is not only essential for success in our personal lives but also in our professional relationships. Whether it's building strong relationships with our colleagues, clients, or customers, confidence plays a crucial role in how we interact with others and how they perceive us.

One of the biggest benefits of confidence in personal and professional relationships is that it helps us to communicate effectively. When we are confident, we are better able to express our thoughts and ideas clearly and assertively, which can help to avoid misunderstandings and ensure that our message is heard and understood.

Confidence also allows us to build stronger and more meaningful connections with others. When we feel confident in ourselves, we are more likely to be open and authentic in our interactions with others, which can help to foster trust and build strong relationships over time.

In addition, confidence can also help to make us more approachable and likable to others. People are naturally drawn to those who are confident and self-assured, and this can help to make it easier to establish connections and build rapport with others, whether in a personal or professional setting.

Another key benefit of confidence in relationships is that it can help us to navigate difficult or challenging situations more effectively. Whether it's having a tough conversation with a colleague or dealing with a challenging customer, confidence can help us to stay calm, focused, and assertive, even in the face of adversity.

At the same time, it's important to remember that confidence should not be confused with arrogance or overconfidence. When we are overconfident or arrogant, we can come across as dismissive or disrespectful of others, which can damage relationships and undermine our credibility.

Instead, the key to building strong relationships through confidence is to find the right balance between assertiveness and empathy. By being assertive and self-assured while also being respectful and empathetic towards others, we can build strong, collaborative relationships that benefit everyone involved.

10: THE BENEFITS OF CONFIDENCE IN PERSONAL AND PROFESSIONAL RELATIONSHIPS

Overall, confidence is a critical ingredient for success in personal and professional relationships. Whether it's building strong connections with others, navigating difficult situations, or simply being more approachable and likable to others, the benefits of confidence are clear. By working to cultivate confidence in ourselves, we can unlock our full potential and transform our relationships in all areas of our lives.

11: The Link Between Confidence and Communication Skills

Effective communication is a key component of success in all aspects of life. Whether it is in the workplace, social situations, or personal relationships, the ability to communicate clearly and confidently is essential. Confidence plays a crucial role in this process, as it allows individuals to express themselves freely and effectively.

When we lack confidence, our communication skills suffer. We may struggle to articulate our thoughts and feelings, and our messages may be misinterpreted or overlooked. On the other hand, when we feel confident, we are more likely to express ourselves clearly and concisely, making it easier for others to understand our message.

Confidence affects our communication skills in many ways. Here are some of the most important:

– Clear communication: When we lack confidence, we may speak too quietly, too quickly, or too hesitantly, making it difficult for others to hear or understand us. When we are confident, we speak clearly and with conviction, making it easier for others to follow our train of thought.

11: THE LINK BETWEEN CONFIDENCE AND COMMU-NICATION SKILLS

– Body language: Our body language communicates as much as our words do. When we lack confidence, we may slouch, avoid eye contact, or fidget nervously, which can undermine our message. When we feel confident, we stand tall, make eye contact, and use gestures to emphasize our points, which helps to reinforce our message.

– Listening skills: Communication is a two-way street, and listening is just as important as speaking. When we lack confidence, we may be so focused on our own thoughts and feelings that we forget to listen to others. When we feel confident, we are more open to hearing what others have to say, which helps us to respond appropriately and build stronger relationships.

– Persuasion: Confidence is essential when it comes to persuading others. Whether it is convincing your boss to give you a promotion, persuading a friend to try a new restaurant, or negotiating a business deal, confidence is key. When we feel confident, we are more persuasive, as we are able to make a compelling case for our point of view.

– Conflict resolution: Conflicts are a normal part of life, but they can be difficult to navigate. When we lack confidence, we may shy away from conflicts or become defensive, which can escalate the situation. When we feel confident, we are better equipped to handle conflicts, as we can stay calm, express ourselves clearly, and work towards a resolution.

In summary, confidence plays a vital role in our communication skills. It allows us to express ourselves clearly, listen attentively, persuade others, and handle conflicts effectively. By working on our confidence, we can improve our communication skills and build stronger, more fulfilling relationships in all aspects of our lives.

12: The Importance of Body Language and Non-Verbal Communication

Communication is a multifaceted process that involves both verbal and nonverbal elements. While the words we use are certainly important, they are only part of the equation. In fact, studies have shown that the majority of our communication is actually conveyed through nonverbal cues such as body language, facial expressions, and tone of voice.

Body language is a particularly important aspect of nonverbal communication, as it can often convey our true feelings and emotions more accurately than our words. For example, if someone is saying one thing but their body language is communicating something different, it can create confusion and mistrust.

So why is body language so important when it comes to confidence? Simply put, it can either enhance or detract from our message. If we are slouching, avoiding eye contact, or fidgeting nervously, it can send the message that we lack confidence and are not comfortable in our own skin. On the other hand, if we stand tall, maintain eye contact, and use open and confident body language, it can convey a sense of self-assuredness and authority.

One of the keys to using body language effectively is to be aware of your own nonverbal cues. This means paying attention to your posture, your facial expressions, and your gestures. If you find that you tend to slouch or look down when you speak, try practicing standing up straight and making eye contact. If you tend to fidget nervously with your hands, try using purposeful gestures to emphasize your points instead.

Another important aspect of body language is mirroring. Mirroring is the process of mimicking the body language of the person you are communicating with, and it can be a powerful tool for building rapport and establishing trust. When we mirror someone's body language, it can create a sense of connection and understanding, which can be particularly helpful in professional or personal relationships.

Of course, it's also important to be mindful of the body language of others. Pay attention to the cues they are sending with their posture, gestures, and expressions. If someone seems closed off or defensive, it may be a sign that they are not comfortable or confident in the situation. On the other hand, if someone is using open and confident body language, it may be a sign that they are feeling self-assured and in control.

Overall, body language and nonverbal communication play a critical role in building confidence and establishing effective communication. By paying attention to your own nonverbal cues and being mindful of the body language of others, you can improve your ability to connect with others and convey a sense of confidence and authority.

13: Confidence and Public Speaking: Tips and Techniques for Success

Introduction:

Public speaking can be intimidating for even the most confident people. It's a skill that requires practice, preparation, and the right mindset. However, mastering public speaking can greatly improve your confidence and open doors to opportunities in your personal and professional life. In this chapter, we will explore the link between confidence and public speaking and provide tips and techniques for success.

The Link Between Confidence and Public Speaking:

Confidence and public speaking are closely linked. When you're confident, you're more likely to speak clearly, engage your audience, and get your message across effectively. On the other hand, when you lack confidence, your body language and tone of voice can betray your nerves, and your message may not come across as effectively. Public speaking can be a daunting task, but with the right mindset, you can turn it into an opportunity to showcase your skills and talents.

13: CONFIDENCE AND PUBLIC SPEAKING: TIPS AND TECHNIQUES FOR SUCCESS

Tips and Techniques for Success:

- Prepare: Preparation is key to successful public speaking. Take the time to research your topic and organize your thoughts. Create an outline or script, and practice your delivery. The more prepared you are, the more confident you will feel.

- Practice: Practice your speech in front of a mirror, record yourself, or present to a small audience. This will help you identify areas where you can improve and build confidence in your delivery.

- Connect with Your Audience: Engage your audience by using eye contact, humor, and relatable stories. This will help you connect with your audience and keep their attention throughout your speech.

- Use Body Language: Your body language can convey confidence and enthusiasm, or nervousness and discomfort. Stand up straight, make eye contact, and use hand gestures to emphasize your points.

- Control Your Breathing: Deep breathing exercises can

help you relax and calm your nerves. Practice deep breathing before your speech to help you stay calm and focused.

– Visualize Success: Visualize yourself delivering a successful speech. Imagine the audience engaging with your message, and feeling confident and proud of your performance.

– Seek Feedback: Ask for feedback from a trusted friend or mentor. They can provide constructive criticism to help you improve and build confidence for future public speaking opportunities.

Conclusion:

Public speaking can be a challenging but rewarding experience. With the right preparation, practice, and mindset, you can develop the confidence and skills necessary to deliver effective speeches. Whether you're giving a presentation at work or delivering a keynote address, use these tips and techniques to help you succeed. Remember, confidence is key to public speaking success, so believe in yourself and your message.

14: Confidence and Networking: How to Make Connections with Ease

Networking can be a daunting experience, especially for those who struggle with confidence. However, building connections and establishing relationships is an important aspect of personal and professional growth. In this chapter, we will explore how to boost confidence and effectively network in various situations.

First, it is important to understand what networking is and why it is important. Networking is the act of meeting and connecting with individuals who share similar interests or professional goals. It can happen in various settings, such as conferences, events, social media platforms, or even casual conversations. Networking provides individuals with the opportunity to build relationships, share ideas and experiences, and potentially collaborate on future projects or opportunities.

However, for many individuals, networking can be an anxiety-provoking experience. This is often due to a lack of confidence in one's social skills or fear of rejection. The good news is that confidence can be developed and improved through practice and intentional effort.

One of the first steps to building confidence in networking situations is to do some research and preparation. Before attending an event or engaging in a networking opportunity, it can be helpful to do some research on the individuals or organizations that will be present. This can provide a sense of familiarity and ease when initiating conversations.

It is also important to prepare an elevator pitch, which is a concise and compelling summary of who you are, what you do, and what your goals are. This can be useful when introducing yourself to new people or when answering the common question, "what do you do?".

Another strategy for building confidence in networking situations is to focus on the other person. This means actively listening to what the other person is saying and asking questions about their interests and goals. This can take the pressure off of oneself and create a more relaxed and enjoyable conversation.

It is also important to practice active listening and engage in positive body language during conversations. This means making eye contact, nodding and smiling, and avoiding distracting behaviors such as checking one's phone or looking around the room.

In addition to in-person networking opportunities, social media platforms can also be a valuable tool for building connections and establishing relationships. It is important to maintain a professional and authentic online presence, and actively engage with individuals or organizations that align with one's interests and goals.

Finally, it is important to remember that networking is not a one-time event, but rather a continuous process of building and maintaining relationships. Following up with individuals after initial conversations or meetings can be a valuable way to solidify connections and potentially lead to future opportunities.

In conclusion, networking is an important aspect of personal and professional growth, but can also be a challenging experience for individuals who struggle with confidence. However, by doing some research and preparation, focusing on the other person, practicing active listening and positive

14: CONFIDENCE AND NETWORKING: HOW TO MAKE CONNECTIONS WITH EASE

body language, and utilizing social media platforms, individuals can build confidence and effectively network in various situations.

15: Navigating Imposter Syndrome: Overcoming Self-Doubt and Achieving Success

Imposter syndrome is a common phenomenon experienced by individuals across all walks of life. It's a condition where an individual feels like they don't deserve their achievements, despite being competent and qualified. Instead, they attribute their success to luck or other external factors, and they fear being exposed as a fraud. This fear of being exposed can lead to a lack of confidence and self-doubt, which can have a significant impact on an individual's ability to reach their full potential.

While imposter syndrome can affect anyone, it's often more prevalent in individuals who are high achievers or in positions of leadership. It's important to recognize the signs of imposter syndrome and learn how to overcome it to build unshakeable confidence and achieve success.

One of the key steps to overcoming imposter syndrome is to recognize that it's a common phenomenon and that many successful people experience it. It's essential to understand that feeling like a fraud doesn't mean that you are one, and it's okay to make mistakes and learn from them.

Another way to overcome imposter syndrome is to focus on your strengths and accomplishments. Keep a list of your achievements and revisit them when you start to doubt yourself. This exercise can help you recognize that you've worked hard to achieve your goals, and you deserve to be where you are.

It's also crucial to challenge negative self-talk and reframe it in a positive light. Instead of focusing on what you can't do or where you fall short, focus on your strengths and what you can do. Don't compare yourself to others, as this can lead to feelings of inadequacy and self-doubt.

Another way to overcome imposter syndrome is to seek support from others. Talk to people you trust about your feelings and concerns. Often, just expressing your thoughts can help you gain a new perspective and find solutions to the challenges you're facing.

Additionally, it's crucial to set realistic goals and expectations for yourself. Instead of striving for perfection, aim for progress. Recognize that everyone makes mistakes and that they are opportunities to learn and grow.

Another way to overcome imposter syndrome is to take risks and step outside your comfort zone. This can help you build confidence in your abilities and realize that you are capable of achieving great things.

Finally, it's essential to practice self-care and prioritize your mental and emotional well-being. Make time for activities that bring you joy and relaxation, such as exercise, meditation, or spending time with loved ones. Taking care of yourself can help you build resilience and overcome imposter syndrome.

In conclusion, imposter syndrome can be a significant obstacle to building confidence and achieving success. However, by recognizing the signs and taking steps to overcome it, you can build unshakeable confidence and reach your full potential. Remember to focus on your strengths, challenge negative self-talk, seek support from others, set realistic goals, take risks, and prioritize self-care. With these strategies, you can navigate imposter syndrome and achieve success in all areas of your life.

16: Building Confidence in the Workplace: Strategies for Career Advancement

In today's highly competitive and fast-paced workplace, confidence is a crucial element for success. It's not only important to have the necessary skills and qualifications but also the confidence to showcase them effectively. When you exude confidence, it reflects positively on your work and can help you build trust with your colleagues and superiors. This chapter will explore some of the strategies for building confidence in the workplace and achieving career advancement.

– Focus on your strengths

It's important to focus on your strengths and to use them to your advantage. When you understand what you are good at, you can capitalize on those strengths and position yourself as an expert in that area. This can help you build confidence in yourself and in others' perception of you.

– Take on new challenges

Taking on new challenges can help you build your confidence and develop new skills. Don't be afraid to step out of your comfort zone and take on projects or tasks that may seem daunting at first. This can help you gain new experiences, learn new skills, and build your confidence in your abilities.

– Seek out feedback

Feedback is essential for growth and improvement, and it can also help build confidence. Seek out feedback from your colleagues and superiors, and be open to constructive criticism. Use this feedback to improve your skills and continue to grow professionally.

– Network

Networking is a great way to build confidence and advance your career. Attend industry events, join professional organizations, and connect with colleagues and mentors. Networking can help you build relationships with people who can offer guidance, support, and opportunities for career advancement.

– Set goals

16: BUILDING CONFIDENCE IN THE WORKPLACE: STRATEGIES FOR CAREER ADVANCEMENT

Setting goals can help you stay focused and motivated in your career. When you set achievable goals, you create a roadmap for success and can measure your progress along the way. This can help build confidence and show that you are making progress toward your career goals.

– Practice self-care

Taking care of yourself is essential for building confidence in the workplace. This includes getting enough sleep, exercise, and eating a healthy diet. When you feel good physically, you are more likely to feel confident and focused in your work.

– Celebrate your successes

It's important to celebrate your successes, no matter how small they may be. Acknowledging your accomplishments can help build your confidence and motivate you to continue to strive for success.

– Learn from your failures

Failure is a natural part of the learning process, and it's important to embrace it and learn from it. When you experience a setback or failure, take the time to reflect on what went wrong and what you can do differently next time. Use this experience to grow and improve, and don't let it damage your confidence.

In conclusion, building confidence in the workplace is essential for career advancement and success. By focusing on your strengths, taking on new challenges, seeking feedback, networking, setting goals, practicing self-care, celebrating your successes, and learning from your failures, you can develop the confidence you need to achieve your career goals. Remember that building confidence takes time and effort, but it's worth the investment in yourself and your future.

17: Overcoming Rejection and Failure: Learning from Setbacks and Bouncing Back Stronger

Introduction

At some point in our lives, we all experience rejection and failure. It could be a job rejection, a failed relationship, or a business venture that didn't work out. Whatever the case may be, rejection and failure can leave us feeling defeated and hopeless. But what if we could learn to overcome these setbacks and turn them into opportunities for growth and success? This chapter explores the importance of overcoming rejection and failure, and provides practical strategies for bouncing back stronger and more resilient than ever before.

The Importance of Overcoming Rejection and Failure

Rejection and failure are inevitable parts of life, but it's how we respond to them that really matters. Those who are able to bounce back from setbacks are often the ones who go on to achieve great success. Consider some of the most successful people in history, from Oprah Winfrey to Thomas Edison to J.K. Rowling. Each of them experienced significant failures and setbacks along the way, but they refused to let those setbacks define them. Instead, they used those experiences as opportunities for growth and learning.

But why is it so important to overcome rejection and failure? For one thing, it builds resilience. Resilient people are able to bounce back from setbacks and remain optimistic about the future. They don't let rejection or failure hold them back from pursuing their goals and dreams. Additionally, overcoming rejection and failure can help us develop a growth mindset. Instead of seeing failure as a reflection of our abilities or worth, we can learn to see it as an opportunity for growth and improvement.

Strategies for Overcoming Rejection and Failure

So how can we learn to overcome rejection and failure? Here are some practical strategies to consider:

– Practice self-compassion: It's easy to beat ourselves up after a failure or rejection. But research shows that self-compassion can actually help us bounce back more quickly. Instead of berating yourself for your mistakes, practice self-compassion by reminding yourself that everyone makes mistakes and that failure is a normal part of the learning process.

— Reframe your mindset: Instead of seeing failure as a reflection of your abilities or worth, reframe your mindset to see it as an opportunity for growth and learning. Ask yourself, "What can I learn from this experience?" or "How can I use this setback to improve in the future?"

— Seek support: Don't be afraid to reach out to friends, family members, or a therapist for support after a setback. Talking to someone about your experience can help you process your emotions and gain a new perspective on the situation.

— Take action: After a setback, it's important to take action towards your goals. This could mean applying for a new job, trying a new approach in your business, or seeking out new opportunities in your personal life. Taking action can help you regain a sense of control and purpose.

— Learn from your mistakes: Take the time to reflect on what went wrong and what you could do differently in the

future. This could mean seeking feedback from others, reading up on best practices in your industry, or simply taking a
step back and analyzing the situation objectively.

Conclusion

Overcoming rejection and failure is never easy, but it's a necessary part of growth and success. By practicing self-compassion, reframing our mindset, seeking support, taking action, and learning from our mistakes, we can bounce back
stronger and more resilient than ever before. Remember,
setbacks are not a reflection of our abilities or worth. They
are simply opportunities for growth and learning. So the
next time you experience a rejection or failure, take a deep
breath, practice self-compassion, and get ready to bounce
back stronger than ever before.

18: Dealing with Criticism: How to Handle Feedback and Constructive Criticism

Constructive criticism is an important tool for personal and professional growth. However, receiving criticism, even when it's constructive, can be difficult and can cause feelings of defensiveness, inadequacy, or even anger. Knowing how to handle feedback in a constructive manner can help you turn negative experiences into opportunities for personal development.

One of the first things to remember when dealing with criticism is to stay calm and try not to take things too personally. Criticism is not a personal attack, but rather an opportunity for improvement. You can't control the criticism you receive, but you can control how you respond to it.

It is also important to keep an open mind when receiving feedback. Listen to what the person is saying and ask clarifying questions if necessary. Take the time to understand their perspective and try to see things from their point of view. This will help you to objectively assess the situation and determine if there is any truth to what they are saying.

18: DEALING WITH CRITICISM: HOW TO HANDLE FEEDBACK AND CONSTRUCTIVE CRITICISM

When receiving criticism, it is important to avoid becoming defensive. Defensiveness can lead to a breakdown in communication and make it difficult to have a productive conversation. Instead, focus on staying calm and responding in a professional and respectful manner.

If the criticism is valid, acknowledge it and take responsibility for your actions. Use the feedback to learn from the experience and make improvements for the future. Remember, making mistakes is a part of the learning process, and it is through mistakes that we grow and improve.

If the criticism is not valid, calmly explain your perspective and why you disagree with their assessment. It's important to do this in a respectful manner and not to attack the other person. By responding in a calm and professional manner, you can help to diffuse the situation and keep the lines of communication open.

Another important aspect of handling criticism is to use it as an opportunity for growth. Take the feedback you receive and use it as a way to learn and improve. Make a plan for how you can implement the feedback in the future and put it into action. By doing this, you are showing that you are receptive to feedback and are committed to improving yourself.

It's also important to remember that not all criticism is constructive. Some people may criticize you in a negative and unhelpful way. In these situations, it's important to assess the situation and determine if the criticism is valid or not. If it is not valid, then it's important to let it go and not let it affect your confidence.

In summary, receiving criticism can be difficult, but it is an opportunity for growth and development. Stay calm, keep an open mind, avoid becoming defensive, take responsibility for your actions, and use the feedback to learn and improve. By doing so, you can turn negative experiences into opportunities for personal growth and development.

19: Confidence and Decision Making: Making Decisions with Clarity and Conviction

Introduction

Every day, we are faced with numerous decisions, both big and small. From deciding what to wear in the morning to making major life-changing choices, our lives are constantly filled with decisions. However, making decisions can be challenging, especially when we are faced with uncertainty or fear of making the wrong choice. Confidence plays a significant role in decision making, as it helps us to make decisions with clarity and conviction. In this chapter, we will explore the link between confidence and decision making, and provide tips and techniques for making decisions with confidence.

The Link Between Confidence and Decision Making

Confidence is essential for making decisions because it helps us to believe in ourselves and our ability to make the right choices. When we lack confidence, we may second-guess ourselves, become indecisive, or rely too heavily on others to make decisions for us. This can lead to a lack of direction in our lives, as well as missed opportunities.

On the other hand, when we have confidence in ourselves and our abilities, we are more likely to make decisions with clarity and conviction. We trust our instincts, rely on our own judgment, and take calculated risks. We are also more likely to learn from our mistakes and use them as opportunities for growth.

Tips for Making Decisions with Confidence

– Clarify Your Values and Priorities

Before making any decision, it's essential to clarify your values and priorities. Ask yourself what's most important to you and what you want to achieve in the long-term. This will help you to make decisions that align with your values and goals, and give you a sense of purpose and direction.

– Gather Information

Gather as much information as possible before making a decision. This includes researching the options available, seeking advice from trusted sources, and considering the potential outcomes of each option. The more information you

have, the better equipped you will be to make an informed
decision.

– Trust Your Instincts

While it's important to gather information and consider the
potential outcomes of each option, don't ignore your instincts. Your gut feelings are often a result of your subconscious processing information that you may not even be
aware of consciously. Trusting your instincts can help you
to make decisions that are aligned with your values and priorities, and that feel right for you.

– Practice Decision-Making

Like any skill, decision-making takes practice. Start by making small decisions on a regular basis, and gradually work
your way up to more significant choices. This will help you
to build your confidence in decision-making and develop
your ability to make choices with clarity and conviction.

– Embrace Failure as a Learning Opportunity

Making mistakes is a natural part of the decision-making
process. Instead of fearing failure, embrace it as an oppor-

tunity to learn and grow. Reflect on your decisions and outcomes, and use them to inform future choices. Remember, failure is not a reflection of your worth or ability, but rather a stepping stone on the path to success.

Conclusion

Confidence is essential for making decisions with clarity and conviction. By clarifying your values and priorities, gathering information, trusting your instincts, practicing decision-making, and embracing failure as a learning opportunity, you can develop your confidence in decision-making and make choices that align with your goals and values. With these tips and techniques, you can navigate the decision-making process with confidence and make the most of every opportunity that comes your way.

20: The Role of Confidence in Leadership: Leading with Confidence and Authenticity

Leadership requires confidence, but not just any kind of confidence. It requires a specific type of confidence that is grounded in authenticity and an understanding of one's own strengths and limitations. Leaders who exude this type of confidence are able to inspire their teams and guide them towards success.

In this chapter, we will explore the role of confidence in leadership, and how leaders can cultivate the kind of confidence that is needed to be successful.

What is Confidence in Leadership?

Confidence in leadership can be defined as the belief in oneself and one's ability to lead others towards success. It is the ability to make decisions with conviction, even in the face of uncertainty or adversity. However, confidence in leadership is not simply about being self-assured or assertive. It is also about being able to inspire and motivate others towards a shared vision.

20: THE ROLE OF CONFIDENCE IN LEADERSHIP: LEADING WITH CONFIDENCE AND AUTHENTICITY

Confidence in leadership is a critical factor in determining a leader's effectiveness. A lack of confidence can result in indecisiveness, reluctance to take risks, and a failure to inspire others. On the other hand, too much confidence can lead to overconfidence, which can result in poor decision-making and a failure to take into account the opinions and perspectives of others.

How to Cultivate Confidence in Leadership

Confidence in leadership can be developed through a combination of self-awareness, experience, and intentional practice. Here are some strategies that leaders can use to cultivate confidence:

– Develop Self-Awareness: Leaders who are self-aware understand their own strengths and limitations. They are able to acknowledge their own weaknesses, and seek out opportunities to improve their skills and knowledge. This type of self-awareness is critical in developing the kind of confidence that is grounded in authenticity.

– Seek Out Experience: Experience is a key factor in developing confidence. Leaders who seek out new challenges and opportunities to learn are able to develop the skills and knowledge necessary to lead effectively. This type of experience also helps leaders to develop a sense of resilience, which is critical in overcoming obstacles and setbacks.

– Embrace Failure: Failure is a natural part of the learning process. Leaders who are able to embrace failure, learn from their mistakes, and move forward with a sense of resilience are more likely to be confident in their ability to lead.

– Practice Confidence-Building Exercises: There are a variety of exercises and techniques that leaders can use to build their confidence. For example, leaders can practice public speaking, engage in role-playing exercises, or engage in visualization exercises to help them develop a sense of confidence.

Leading with Authenticity

Authenticity is a critical component of confidence in leadership. Leaders who are authentic are able to connect with their teams on a deeper level, and inspire them towards a shared vision. Authenticity requires a deep understanding of one's own values, strengths, and weaknesses, and a willingness to be vulnerable and honest with others.

Leaders who lead with authenticity are able to build trust with their teams, and create a sense of psychological safety that allows team members to feel comfortable sharing their opinions and ideas. This type of environment is critical for fostering innovation and creativity, and ultimately, achieving success.

Final Thoughts

Confidence in leadership is a critical factor in determining a leader's effectiveness. However, confidence must be grounded in authenticity and an understanding of one's own strengths and limitations. Leaders who cultivate this type of confidence are able to inspire and motivate their teams towards success, and ultimately, achieve their goals. By developing self-awareness, seeking out experience, embracing failure, and practicing confidence-building exercises, leaders can cultivate the kind of confidence that is needed to lead with authenticity and achieve success.

21: Overcoming Social Anxiety: Tips and Techniques for Social Situations

Introduction:

Social anxiety is a common condition that can cause individuals to feel extreme discomfort in social situations. It can be a debilitating experience that can affect people's quality of life, including their relationships and careers. However, it is important to know that social anxiety is treatable and can be overcome. In this chapter, we will discuss some tips and techniques for overcoming social anxiety and gaining confidence in social situations.

Understanding Social Anxiety:

Social anxiety is a psychological condition that causes individuals to experience significant fear and discomfort in social situations. People with social anxiety often fear being judged, evaluated, or scrutinized by others. They may also fear embarrassing themselves or appearing incompetent. As a result, they may avoid social situations or experience significant distress in these situations.

21: OVERCOMING SOCIAL ANXIETY: TIPS AND TECHNIQUES FOR SOCIAL SITUATIONS

Social anxiety can manifest in various ways, including physical symptoms such as sweating, trembling, or blushing. It can also cause negative thoughts and self-criticism, which can further exacerbate the condition.

Tips for Overcoming Social Anxiety:

– Challenge Negative Thoughts: Negative thoughts can contribute to social anxiety. Challenging these thoughts can help individuals gain a more realistic perspective of themselves and the situation. It can be helpful to ask yourself if the thoughts are based on facts or assumptions. Try to find evidence to support or refute these thoughts.

– Gradual Exposure: Gradually exposing oneself to social situations can help individuals become more comfortable in these situations. Start with small, manageable social situations and gradually work up to more challenging situations.

– Practice Mindfulness: Mindfulness can help individuals stay present and focused in social situations. Practice deep breathing exercises or visualization techniques before and during social situations to help stay calm and centered.

21: OVERCOMING SOCIAL ANXIETY: TIPS AND TECHNIQUES FOR SOCIAL SITUATIONS

– Positive Self-Talk: Positive self-talk can help individuals build confidence and self-esteem. Focus on positive affirmations and remind yourself of past successes and accomplishments.

– Seek Professional Help: If social anxiety is significantly impacting one's quality of life, seeking professional help can be beneficial. A therapist can provide support, guidance, and tools for managing social anxiety.

Techniques for Social Situations:

– Preparation: Prepare for social situations by setting goals, researching the event, and planning conversation starters. Having a plan can help reduce anxiety and increase confidence.

– Active Listening: Focus on listening to others during conversations. This can help individuals stay present and engaged in the conversation, rather than focusing on their own anxiety.

– Visualization: Visualize positive outcomes of social situations. This can help individuals feel more confident and prepared for social situations.

– Practice: Practice social skills in low-pressure situations, such as with family or friends. This can help individuals build confidence and improve social skills.

Conclusion:

Social anxiety can be a challenging condition to overcome, but with the right tools and techniques, it is possible to gain confidence and feel more comfortable in social situations. Challenging negative thoughts, gradual exposure, mindfulness, positive self-talk, and seeking professional help are all effective ways to manage social anxiety. Preparation, active listening, visualization, and practice are all techniques that can be used in social situations to increase confidence and reduce anxiety. With time and practice, individuals can overcome social anxiety and enjoy more fulfilling social interactions.

22: Building Confidence in Dating and Relationships

Dating and relationships can be a source of great joy, but they can also be challenging and anxiety-inducing. Whether you're single and looking for love, or in a committed relationship, building confidence in yourself and your interactions with others can help you create fulfilling and healthy connections with those around you. In this chapter, we'll explore proven strategies and expert insights to help you build confidence in dating and relationships.

Understanding Your Own Worth

Confidence begins with a deep understanding of your own worth. When you believe in yourself and your own value, it becomes easier to approach others with a sense of self-assurance and positivity. Unfortunately, many of us struggle with self-doubt and negative self-talk, which can make it difficult to build confidence in relationships.

One way to combat these feelings is to actively work on building a positive self-image. This can include practices like daily affirmations, meditation, or journaling, where you take time to focus on your strengths and accomplishments.

It can also be helpful to surround yourself with people who support and encourage you, and to take on challenges that help you grow and stretch beyond your comfort zone.

In addition to building a positive self-image, it's important to understand your own values and priorities when it comes to relationships. What are the qualities that you're looking for in a partner? What do you need to feel fulfilled in a relationship? By taking time to reflect on these questions, you can build confidence in your own ability to navigate the dating world and create the kind of relationship that you want.

Overcoming Fear and Anxiety

One of the biggest obstacles to building confidence in dating and relationships is fear and anxiety. Whether you're afraid of rejection, worried about making a mistake, or anxious about opening up to someone else, these feelings can prevent you from taking risks and putting yourself out there.

To overcome these fears, it's important to first acknowledge and accept them. It's natural to feel nervous or anxious when it comes to relationships, and recognizing these feelings can help you move past them. From there, you can work on building skills and strategies to manage your anxiety, such as deep breathing exercises, mindfulness techniques, or seeking professional support.

Another important strategy for overcoming fear and anxiety is to take action. Rather than avoiding situations that make you uncomfortable, try to face them head-on. For example, if you're nervous about asking someone out, try to approach them in a low-pressure setting, like a group outing or casual conversation. By taking small steps and building up your confidence gradually, you can develop the skills and resilience you need to navigate more challenging situations in the future.

Communication and Boundaries

Another key aspect of building confidence in relationships is learning how to communicate effectively and set healthy boundaries. This can be especially important when it comes to dating, where miscommunications and mixed signals can lead to confusion and hurt feelings.

One important aspect of communication is being clear and direct about your intentions and expectations. If you're looking for a committed relationship, make sure that your partner knows this from the outset. Similarly, if you're not interested in pursuing a relationship, be honest and upfront about your feelings. By being clear and direct, you can avoid misunderstandings and ensure that both you and your partner are on the same page.

Setting healthy boundaries is also crucial for building confidence in relationships. This can include boundaries around physical intimacy, communication, or personal space. By setting and enforcing boundaries, you can ensure that your needs and values are respected, and create a sense of safety and trust in your relationships.

Practicing Self-Care

Finally, building confidence in relationships requires a commitment to self-care and personal growth. This can include practices like exercise, healthy eating, and getting enough sleep, which can help you feel physically and emotionally strong. It can also include hobbies and activities that bring you joy and fulfillment, such as spending time with friends, pursuing creative interests, or volunteering in your community.

Self-care can also involve setting aside time to reflect on your own emotional needs and wellbeing. This can include practices like journaling, meditation, or therapy, where you take time to explore your thoughts and feelings in a safe and supportive environment. By prioritizing your own self-care, you can build resilience and a sense of inner strength that can help you navigate the ups and downs of relationships with greater ease.

Conclusion

Building confidence in dating and relationships requires a commitment to self-discovery, self-care, and personal growth. By understanding your own worth, overcoming fear and anxiety, practicing effective communication and setting healthy boundaries, and prioritizing your own self-care, you can create fulfilling and healthy connections with those around you.

Remember that building confidence is a process, and that it's okay to make mistakes and face setbacks along the way. By approaching dating and relationships with a sense of curiosity and openness, and by staying true to your own values and priorities, you can create relationships that bring

you joy, fulfillment, and a deep sense of connection with
others.

23: The Importance of Boundaries in Building Confidence

Boundaries are essential for building confidence and creating a fulfilling life. They define our personal limits and values, and help us establish healthy relationships with ourselves and others. In this chapter, we'll explore the importance of boundaries in building confidence, and provide strategies for setting and maintaining them in all areas of your life.

Understanding Boundaries

Boundaries are the invisible lines that separate us from others. They can be physical, emotional, or psychological, and they help us establish a sense of self and a clear understanding of our personal limits. When our boundaries are respected, we feel safe, secure, and in control of our lives. When they are violated, we may feel anxious, vulnerable, or powerless.

There are many different types of boundaries, but some of the most common include:

– Physical boundaries, which involve our physical space and

the extent to which we allow others to invade it.

– Emotional boundaries, which involve our feelings and the extent to which we allow others to influence them.

– Psychological boundaries, which involve our thoughts and beliefs, and the extent to which we allow others to challenge or change them.

Establishing boundaries is important because it helps us create a sense of self and personal identity. When we know where we stand, we can better understand our own needs and priorities, and we can take steps to protect them. Conversely, when we lack clear boundaries, we may feel uncertain or insecure in our relationships, and we may struggle to assert ourselves or advocate for our own needs.

Setting Healthy Boundaries

Setting healthy boundaries involves being clear and assertive about our needs and expectations. It requires us to take responsibility for our own feelings and actions, and to communicate them clearly to others. Some strategies for setting healthy boundaries include:

– Identify your own needs and values. Before you can establish healthy boundaries, you need to know what you want and need from your relationships. Take time to reflect on your own values and priorities, and be clear about what you are and are not willing to tolerate from others.

– Communicate your boundaries clearly and assertively. When setting boundaries, it's important to be clear and direct about your needs and expectations. Use "I" statements to express your feelings, and avoid blaming or accusing others.

– Stick to your boundaries. Once you've established your boundaries, it's important to stick to them. This may mean saying "no" to certain requests, or being firm in your expectations for how others treat you.

– Be willing to compromise. While it's important to stick to your boundaries, it's also important to be flexible and willing to compromise when appropriate. Consider the needs and feelings of others, and be open to finding solutions that work for everyone involved.

Maintaining Boundaries

23: THE IMPORTANCE OF BOUNDARIES IN BUILDING CONFIDENCE

Maintaining healthy boundaries is an ongoing process that requires vigilance and self-awareness. Some strategies for maintaining healthy boundaries include:

– Regular self-reflection. Take time to reflect on your own feelings and experiences, and be mindful of any situations or relationships that may be violating your boundaries.

– Practice self-care. Taking care of yourself, both physically and emotionally, can help you maintain your boundaries and feel more confident in your relationships.

– Seek support when needed. If you find that your boundaries are being violated or that you're struggling to maintain them, don't be afraid to seek support from friends, family, or a therapist.

– Be open to learning and growing. Boundaries are not set in stone, and they may change as you grow and evolve as a person. Be open to learning and growing, and be willing to adjust your boundaries as needed.

Conclusion

Building confidence requires a strong sense of self and a

clear understanding of your own needs and values. Setting healthy boundaries is an essential part of this process, as it helps us establish a clear sense of self and personal identity, and create healthy and fulfilling relationships with others.

By identifying your own needs and values, communicating your boundaries clearly and assertively, sticking to your boundaries, and being willing to compromise when appropriate, you can establish healthy boundaries in all areas of your life.

Maintaining healthy boundaries requires ongoing self-reflection, self-care, and a willingness to learn and grow. By seeking support when needed and being open to adjusting your boundaries as necessary, you can continue to build confidence and create a life that is fulfilling and true to your own values and priorities.

Remember that boundaries are essential for building confidence and creating healthy relationships, and that it's okay to set and enforce them. By doing so, you can create a life that is authentic, fulfilling, and truly your own.

24: Building Confidence in Parenting: Raising Confident Children

Parenting is one of the most challenging and rewarding experiences in life. As a parent, you play a critical role in shaping your child's self-esteem, confidence, and overall well-being. In this chapter, we'll explore strategies for building confidence in parenting and raising confident children.

The Importance of Confidence in Children

Confidence is an essential trait that can help children thrive in all areas of life. Confident children are more likely to take on new challenges, pursue their interests and passions, and develop healthy relationships with others. They are also more likely to have a positive self-image and a strong sense of personal identity.

On the other hand, children who lack confidence may struggle with self-doubt, anxiety, and low self-esteem. They may be less likely to take risks or pursue their goals, and may have difficulty forming healthy relationships with others.

24: BUILDING CONFIDENCE IN PARENTING: RAISING CONFIDENT CHILDREN

As a parent, you play a critical role in helping your child build confidence and self-esteem. By providing a supportive and nurturing environment, you can help your child develop a strong sense of self and the confidence to pursue their dreams and goals.

Strategies for Building Confidence in Parenting

– Provide a safe and nurturing environment. Children need to feel safe and secure in order to build confidence. As a parent, it's important to create a nurturing and supportive environment where your child feels loved, valued, and accepted.

– Encourage exploration and curiosity. Children are naturally curious and love to explore their environment. Encourage your child's natural curiosity by providing opportunities for exploration and discovery. This can include trips to the park, visits to museums or other educational venues, or simply spending time outdoors.

– Praise effort, not just achievement. Children need to feel valued and recognized for their efforts, not just their achievements. When your child works hard to accomplish something, be sure to acknowledge and praise their efforts.

– Model confidence and resilience. Children learn by example, so it's important to model confidence and resilience in your own life. Show your child how to handle challenges and setbacks with grace and resilience, and demonstrate a positive attitude and mindset.

– Encourage independence. As children grow and develop, they need to feel a sense of independence and autonomy. Encourage your child to make their own decisions and take responsibility for their actions, and provide opportunities for them to practice independence in a safe and supportive environment.

– Foster a growth mindset. A growth mindset is the belief that abilities and intelligence can be developed through hard work and perseverance. Encourage your child to adopt a growth mindset by praising their effort, providing opportunities for learning and growth, and helping them see the value in taking on new challenges.

– Emphasize the importance of self-care. Self-care is an important part of building confidence and self-esteem. Teach your child the importance of taking care of themselves, both physically and emotionally, and provide opportunities for them to practice self-care in their daily lives.

Conclusion

Building confidence in parenting is essential for raising confident and resilient children. By providing a safe and nurturing environment, encouraging exploration and curiosity, praising effort, modeling confidence and resilience, fostering independence, promoting a growth mindset, and emphasizing the importance of self-care, you can help your child develop a strong sense of self and the confidence to pursue their goals and dreams.

Remember that building confidence is a process, and that it takes time and effort to cultivate. As a parent, you play a critical role in shaping your child's self-esteem and confidence, and by providing a supportive and nurturing environment, you can help your child develop the skills and mindset they need to thrive in all areas of life.

25: The Connection Between Confidence and Health and Wellness

When it comes to living a healthy and fulfilling life, confidence plays a crucial role. Confidence can affect your physical health, mental well-being, and overall quality of life. In this chapter, we'll explore the connection between confidence and health and wellness and provide strategies for building confidence to improve your overall well-being.

The Relationship Between Confidence and Health

Confidence is closely linked to physical health. Studies have shown that people who have high levels of self-confidence are more likely to take care of their physical health. They are more likely to exercise regularly, eat a healthy diet, and avoid unhealthy behaviors such as smoking and excessive alcohol consumption.

In addition, confidence can help reduce stress and anxiety, which are known to have negative effects on physical health. When you are confident, you are better equipped to handle stress and manage your emotions, which can help prevent the development of chronic health conditions.

25: THE CONNECTION BETWEEN CONFIDENCE AND HEALTH AND WELLNESS

The Relationship Between Confidence and Mental Health

Confidence also plays an important role in mental health. People who lack confidence may struggle with self-doubt, anxiety, and depression, which can have a negative impact on their overall well-being.

On the other hand, people who have high levels of self-confidence are more likely to have positive self-esteem, a strong sense of identity, and a positive outlook on life. They are better able to handle stress and cope with challenges, which can help prevent the development of mental health conditions.

Strategies for Building Confidence to Improve Health and Wellness

– Practice Self-Care. Self-care is essential for building confidence and improving overall well-being. Make time for activities that make you feel good, such as exercise, meditation, or spending time with loved ones. Prioritize rest and relaxation, and be sure to take care of your physical and emotional needs.

25: THE CONNECTION BETWEEN CONFIDENCE AND HEALTH AND WELLNESS

– Set Realistic Goals. Setting realistic goals can help boost confidence and provide a sense of accomplishment. Start small and work your way up to more challenging goals. Celebrate your successes along the way, and don't be too hard on yourself if you experience setbacks.

– Challenge Negative Self-Talk. Negative self-talk can undermine confidence and contribute to feelings of self-doubt and anxiety. Challenge negative self-talk by replacing it with positive affirmations and focusing on your strengths and accomplishments.

– Take Risks. Taking risks can help build confidence and provide opportunities for growth and learning. Start by taking small risks, such as trying a new hobby or speaking up in a meeting. As you build confidence, you can take on bigger challenges and pursue your goals and dreams.

– Surround Yourself with Supportive People. Surrounding yourself with supportive people can help boost confidence and provide a sense of community. Seek out people who are positive, encouraging, and supportive of your goals and aspirations.

– Practice Mindfulness. Mindfulness can help reduce stress and anxiety and promote feelings of calm and relaxation. Practice mindfulness techniques such as deep breathing, meditation, or yoga to help build confidence and improve overall well-being.

Conclusion

Confidence is a crucial component of health and wellness. By taking care of yourself, setting realistic goals, challenging negative self-talk, taking risks, surrounding yourself with supportive people, and practicing mindfulness, you can build confidence and improve your physical and mental well-being.

Remember that building confidence is a process, and it takes time and effort to cultivate. Be patient with yourself and celebrate your successes along the way. With dedication and perseverance, you can unlock your inner potential and transform your life with unshakeable confidence.

26: Mindfulness and Meditation: Techniques for Cultivating Inner Peace and Confidence

Introduction

In today's fast-paced and high-stress world, it is easy to feel overwhelmed, anxious, and insecure. We often find ourselves struggling with negative thoughts, limiting beliefs, and self-doubt, which can hold us back from reaching our full potential and living a fulfilling life. Confidence is essential to success in every aspect of life, but building and maintaining it can be challenging.

One powerful tool for cultivating inner peace and building confidence is mindfulness and meditation. These techniques have been used for centuries in various cultures and traditions to improve mental and emotional well-being, reduce stress, and enhance overall quality of life. In this chapter, we will explore the benefits of mindfulness and meditation and provide you with practical techniques for incorporating them into your daily routine.

Understanding Mindfulness and Meditation

26: MINDFULNESS AND MEDITATION: TECHNIQUES FOR CULTIVATING INNER PEACE AND CONFIDENCE

Mindfulness and meditation are often used interchangeably, but they are distinct practices with unique benefits. Mindfulness is the practice of paying attention to the present moment, without judgment or distraction. It involves being fully present and aware of your thoughts, feelings, and sensations, as well as the environment around you. Meditation, on the other hand, is a mental exercise that involves focusing your attention on a specific object or activity, such as your breath or a mantra.

Both mindfulness and meditation have been shown to have a range of mental, emotional, and physical benefits. For example, they can reduce stress and anxiety, improve focus and concentration, increase self-awareness and emotional intelligence, and enhance overall well-being. Moreover, they can help you develop a greater sense of inner peace, clarity, and confidence.

Practical Techniques for Cultivating Inner Peace and Confidence

There are many different techniques for practicing mindfulness and meditation, and the key is to find the ones that work best for you. Here are some practical strategies to get you started:

– Mindful Breathing

One of the simplest and most effective mindfulness techniques is mindful breathing. To practice this technique, find a quiet place where you can sit comfortably without any distractions. Then, focus your attention on your breath, noticing the sensation of the air moving in and out of your body. If your mind starts to wander, gently bring your attention back to your breath.

Practicing mindful breathing regularly can help you reduce stress and anxiety, improve focus and concentration, and increase self-awareness.

– Body Scan Meditation

Body scan meditation is a technique that involves focusing your attention on different parts of your body, from your toes to your head, and noticing any sensations or feelings you experience. To practice this technique, find a quiet place where you can lie down comfortably. Then, start by focusing your attention on your toes and gradually move up your body, noticing any sensations or tension you feel. If you notice any tension or discomfort, try to relax that area and breathe deeply.

Body scan meditation can help you become more aware of your body, reduce physical tension, and improve overall relaxation and well-being.

– Loving-Kindness Meditation

Loving-kindness meditation is a practice that involves cultivating feelings of love, compassion, and kindness towards yourself and others. To practice this technique, find a quiet place where you can sit comfortably. Then, visualize yourself and repeat phrases of loving-kindness to yourself, such as "may I be happy, may I be healthy, may I be at peace." After a few minutes, visualize someone you love and repeat the same phrases to them. Then, visualize someone you have difficulty with and repeat the phrases to them.

Loving-kindness meditation can help you develop a greater sense of self-compassion and empathy, reduce negative self-talk, and improve relationships with others.

26: MINDFULNESS AND MEDITATION: TECHNIQUES FOR CULTIVATING INNER PEACE AND CONFIDENCE

– Mindful Walking

Mindful walking is a technique that involves paying attention to the present moment while walking, without any distractions or judgments. To practice this technique, find a quiet place where you can walk comfortably, such as a park or a beach. Start by taking a few deep breaths and focusing your attention on your feet as they make contact with the ground. Then, as you start to walk, notice the sensation of your feet lifting and landing, the movement of your legs and arms, and the surroundings around you.

Practicing mindful walking regularly can help you reduce stress and anxiety, improve focus and concentration, and increase overall physical activity.

– Mindful Eating

Mindful eating is a technique that involves paying attention to the present moment while eating, without any distractions or judgments. To practice this technique, choose a quiet place where you can eat without interruptions, such as a table at home or a park bench. Then, before starting to eat, take a moment to observe the food on your plate, noticing its colors, textures, and smells. Then, take a bite and savor the flavors and sensations, noticing how the food feels in your mouth and how it affects your body.

Practicing mindful eating can help you develop a healthier relationship with food, reduce overeating, and improve digestion and overall well-being.

– Mindful Communication

Mindful communication is a technique that involves paying attention to the present moment while communicating with others, without any distractions or judgments. To practice this technique, start by being fully present and attentive to the person you are talking to, giving them your full attention and listening actively. Then, try to be aware of your own thoughts and emotions, and how they may be affecting the conversation. Finally, try to express yourself clearly and respectfully, without judging or criticizing the other person.

Practicing mindful communication can help you improve relationships with others, reduce misunderstandings and conflicts, and develop a greater sense of empathy and understanding.

26: MINDFULNESS AND MEDITATION: TECHNIQUES FOR CULTIVATING INNER PEACE AND CONFIDENCE

Conclusion

Mindfulness and meditation are powerful techniques for cultivating inner peace and building confidence. By practicing these techniques regularly, you can develop a greater sense of self-awareness, reduce stress and anxiety, and enhance overall well-being. Moreover, you can use mindfulness and meditation to overcome limiting beliefs and negative thought patterns, and develop a more positive and empowering mindset. So, take some time each day to practice mindfulness and meditation, and see how it can transform your life.

27: The Role of Gratitude in Building Confidence

Introduction

Gratitude is a powerful emotion that can have a profound impact on our mental and emotional well-being. When we practice gratitude, we focus on the positive aspects of our lives and acknowledge the things we have to be thankful for, rather than dwelling on the negative. Gratitude can help us build confidence by shifting our perspective, increasing our resilience, and fostering a greater sense of connection with others. In this chapter, we will explore the role of gratitude in building confidence and how you can cultivate a grateful mindset.

The Benefits of Gratitude

Research has shown that practicing gratitude can have numerous benefits for our mental and emotional well-being. Here are just a few of the ways that gratitude can benefit us:

– Improved mood: When we focus on the positive aspects of our lives, it can help to improve our mood and increase feelings of happiness and contentment.

– Reduced stress: Gratitude can help to reduce stress and anxiety by shifting our focus away from negative thoughts and emotions.

– Increased resilience: Practicing gratitude can help us to develop greater resilience and cope more effectively with challenges and setbacks.

– Better relationships: Expressing gratitude towards others can strengthen our relationships and foster a greater sense of connection and empathy.

– Improved physical health: Gratitude has been linked to better physical health, including improved sleep, lower blood pressure, and reduced inflammation.

Cultivating Gratitude

Now that we understand the benefits of gratitude, how can we cultivate a grateful mindset? Here are some strategies you can use to practice gratitude:

– Keep a gratitude journal: One of the simplest ways to practice gratitude is to keep a daily gratitude journal. Each day, write down three things you are grateful for. These can

be small things, like a good cup of coffee or a beautiful sunset, or larger things, like a supportive partner or a fulfilling
job.

– Express gratitude to others: Another way to cultivate gratitude is to express it to others. Take a few minutes each day
to thank someone in your life for something they have done,
whether it's a friend who listened to you vent or a colleague
who helped you with a project.

– Practice mindfulness: Mindfulness can help us to become
more aware of the present moment and the things we have
to be grateful for. Try taking a few minutes each day to focus on your breath and notice the things around you that
you are grateful for.

– Reframe negative thoughts: When we are faced with negative thoughts or situations, we can try to reframe them in a
more positive light. For example, instead of dwelling on the
traffic jam that made you late for work, focus on the fact
that you have a job to go to.

– Volunteer or give back: Giving back to others can be a
powerful way to cultivate gratitude. Consider volunteering

at a local charity or donating to a cause that you care about.

Using Gratitude to Build Confidence

Now that we know how to cultivate gratitude, how can we use it to build confidence? Here are some ways that gratitude can help to boost our confidence:

— Shifting our focus: When we practice gratitude, we shift our focus away from the negative and towards the positive aspects of our lives. This can help us to feel more optimistic and confident about our future.

— Increasing resilience: Gratitude can help us to develop greater resilience in the face of challenges and setbacks. By focusing on the things we are grateful for, we can build a stronger sense of inner strength and resourcefulness.

— Enhancing self-esteem: When we focus on the positive aspects of ourselves and our lives, it can help to enhance our self-esteem and self-worth.

— Fostering connection: Gratitude can help us to build stronger connections with others, which can in turn boost our confidence. When we feel supported and connected to others, we are more likely to feel confident in ourselves and our abilities.

– Countering limiting beliefs: When we practice gratitude, we challenge limiting beliefs that may be holding us back. For example, if we are feeling down about our job, focusing on the aspects of our work that we are grateful for can help us to see the value in what we do and build confidence in our abilities.

Practicing gratitude regularly can help us to build a more positive and confident mindset. By cultivating gratitude, we can shift our perspective and focus on the positive aspects of our lives, which can help us to feel more confident and resilient in the face of challenges.

Conclusion

Gratitude is a powerful tool for building confidence and enhancing our overall well-being. By focusing on the positive aspects of our lives and expressing gratitude towards others, we can cultivate a more positive and optimistic mindset. Gratitude can help us to build resilience, enhance our self-esteem, and foster stronger connections with others. By

27: THE ROLE OF GRATITUDE IN BUILDING CONFIDENCE

making gratitude a regular part of our lives, we can unlock our inner potential and build the unshakeable confidence we need to succeed in all areas of our lives.

28: Overcoming Perfectionism: Embracing Your Imperfections and Building Confidence

Introduction

Perfectionism is the belief that one must be perfect or do things perfectly in order to be successful, accepted, or loved. It is a common trait among high achievers, but can also lead to self-doubt, anxiety, and low self-esteem. In this chapter, we will explore the negative impact of perfectionism on our confidence, and strategies for overcoming perfectionism to embrace our imperfections and build greater confidence in ourselves.

The Negative Impact of Perfectionism on Confidence

Perfectionism can have a significant impact on our confidence in a number of ways:

– Fear of failure: Perfectionists often fear failure more than anything else, which can lead to self-doubt and anxiety. This fear can prevent us from taking risks and trying new things, limiting our opportunities for growth and success.

28: OVERCOMING PERFECTIONISM: EMBRACING YOUR IMPERFECTIONS AND BUILDING CONFIDENCE

– Unrealistic expectations: Perfectionists set extremely high standards for themselves, often impossible to achieve. When we inevitably fall short of these standards, we can feel like we are not good enough, leading to a cycle of self-doubt and low self-esteem.

– Comparison with others: Perfectionists tend to compare themselves to others, focusing on their flaws and shortcomings rather than their own strengths and accomplishments. This can lead to feelings of inadequacy and low self-esteem, as we feel we can never measure up to others.

– Inability to enjoy success: Perfectionists often struggle to enjoy their successes because they are always striving for more. This can lead to a lack of satisfaction and fulfillment in our accomplishments, leading to a constant need for validation and approval from others.

Strategies for Overcoming Perfectionism and Building Confidence

– Challenge your self-talk: Perfectionists often have a critical inner voice that reinforces negative beliefs about themselves. To overcome this, challenge your negative self-talk and replace it with positive affirmations. Focus on your strengths and accomplishments, and remind yourself that it is okay to make mistakes.

— Set realistic goals: Instead of setting impossible standards for yourself, set realistic goals that are achievable. This will help you to build confidence in your abilities and feel a sense of accomplishment when you reach your goals.

— Practice self-compassion: Instead of being harsh on your-self when you make mistakes, practice self-compassion. Treat yourself with kindness and understanding, just as you would a good friend.

— Embrace imperfection: Embrace your imperfections and recognize that they are what make you unique and special. Embrace the learning opportunities that come from making mistakes, and celebrate your successes, no matter how small.

— Focus on the process, not just the outcome: Perfectionists often focus solely on the end result, rather than the journey that gets them there. By focusing on the process and the progress you are making, you can build greater confidence and a sense of accomplishment, even if the outcome is not perfect.

Conclusion

Perfectionism can be a major obstacle to building confidence and achieving our goals. By embracing imperfection, setting realistic goals, practicing self-compassion, and focusing on the process rather than just the outcome, we can overcome perfectionism and build greater confidence in ourselves. Remember, it is our imperfections that make us unique and special, and it is okay to make mistakes along the way. Embrace your imperfections and focus on your strengths, and you will be well on your way to building unshakeable confidence in all areas of your life.

29: The Connection Between Confidence and Creativity

Introduction

Confidence and creativity are often seen as separate qualities, but they are actually closely connected. Confidence can help to fuel creativity, and creative pursuits can help to build confidence. In this chapter, we will explore the relationship between confidence and creativity, and how each can help to enhance the other.

The Relationship Between Confidence and Creativity

Confidence can be a major factor in creativity. When we are confident in our abilities, we are more likely to take risks and try new things. We are also more likely to push past obstacles and setbacks, and persevere in the face of challenges. This confidence can lead to greater creativity, as we are more willing to experiment and explore new ideas.

On the other hand, creativity can also help to build confidence. When we engage in creative pursuits, we are using our imagination and expressing ourselves in unique ways. This can help us to build a sense of self-expression and identity, which can in turn boost our confidence. Additionally, when we create something we are proud of, it can give us a sense of accomplishment and validation, further boosting our confidence.

Strategies for Boosting Confidence Through Creativity

– Try new creative pursuits: Trying new creative pursuits can help to build confidence and increase creativity. This can include anything from painting and drawing to writing and music. The key is to try something new and challenging, and to allow yourself to make mistakes along the way.

– Embrace imperfection: When engaging in creative pursuits, it is important to embrace imperfection. Creativity is not about creating something perfect, but about expressing yourself in unique and meaningful ways. Allow yourself to make mistakes and learn from them, and focus on the process rather than the end result.

– Take risks: Taking risks is a major component of creativity and can help to boost confidence. This can include trying new techniques, experimenting with different materials, or sharing your work with others. By taking risks and pushing yourself out of your comfort zone, you can build greater confidence in your abilities.

– Collaborate with others: Collaboration can be a great way to build confidence and increase creativity. By working with others, you can bounce ideas off each other and receive feedback and support. This can help to build confidence in your abilities and generate new and innovative ideas.

– Celebrate your successes: When you create something you are proud of, take time to celebrate your success. This can help to boost your confidence and motivate you to continue creating and exploring new ideas.

Conclusion

Confidence and creativity are closely connected, and can both be enhanced through the other. By engaging in creative pursuits, taking risks, collaborating with others, and celebrating our successes, we can build greater confidence in ourselves and increase our creativity. Remember, creativity is not about creating something perfect, but about expressing yourself in unique and meaningful ways. Allow yourself to embrace imperfection and take risks, and you will be well on your way to building unshakeable confidence and unlocking your full creative potential.

30: Overcoming Procrastination: Strategies for Taking Action and Building Confidence

Introduction

Procrastination is a common challenge that can impact our ability to achieve our goals and build confidence. When we procrastinate, we put off taking action on important tasks and responsibilities, which can lead to feelings of guilt, anxiety, and stress. In this chapter, we will explore the reasons why we procrastinate and provide strategies for overcoming procrastination and building confidence.

Why Do We Procrastinate?

There are several reasons why we may procrastinate, including:

– Fear of failure: When we are afraid of failing, we may put off taking action on important tasks. Procrastination can provide a temporary relief from the fear of failure, but it ultimately reinforces our belief that we are not capable of achieving our goals.

– Lack of motivation: When we lack motivation, we may struggle to take action on important tasks. This can be due to a lack of interest in the task, a lack of confidence in our abilities, or feeling overwhelmed by the task.

– Perfectionism: When we have perfectionistic tendencies, we may put off taking action until we feel we can do the task perfectly. This can lead to a cycle of procrastination, as we may never feel ready to take action.

– Lack of structure or accountability: When we lack structure or accountability, we may struggle to prioritize tasks and take action. This can lead to procrastination as we may feel unsure of where to start or what to do next.

Strategies for Overcoming Procrastination

– Identify the underlying cause: The first step in overcoming procrastination is to identify the underlying cause. This may involve reflecting on your beliefs, attitudes, and habits, and identifying any patterns that may be contributing to your procrastination.

– Break tasks into smaller, manageable steps: Often, procrastination can be a result of feeling overwhelmed by a task. By breaking tasks into smaller, manageable steps, you can make the task feel more achievable and reduce the likelihood of procrastinating.

– Set specific goals and deadlines: Setting specific goals and deadlines can help to increase motivation and accountability. Make sure your goals are realistic and achievable, and break them down into smaller milestones if necessary.

– Use positive self-talk: When we are feeling overwhelmed or anxious about a task, it can be helpful to use positive self-talk to build confidence and reduce stress. Affirmations such as "I am capable of achieving my goals" and "I am taking positive steps towards my success" can help to reframe negative self-talk and build confidence.

– Create a supportive environment: Creating a supportive environment can help to reduce distractions and increase focus. This may involve setting up a dedicated workspace, turning off notifications on your phone, or seeking support from friends or family.

– Reward yourself for taking action: When you take action

on a task, reward yourself with something that you enjoy. This can help to reinforce positive behaviors and build motivation.

Conclusion

Procrastination can be a major obstacle to building confidence and achieving our goals. By identifying the underlying causes of procrastination and implementing strategies such as breaking tasks into smaller steps, setting specific goals and deadlines, using positive self-talk, creating a supportive environment, and rewarding yourself for taking action, you can overcome procrastination and build greater confidence in your abilities. Remember, taking action is the key to building confidence and achieving your goals. Don't let procrastination hold you back from unlocking your inner potential and transforming your life.

31: Building Confidence in Financial Matters: Tips and Techniques for Financial Success

Money is one of the most common sources of anxiety and stress for people, and it's no wonder why. From paying bills and managing debt to investing and saving for retirement, financial matters can be complex and overwhelming. But financial success isn't just about making more money; it's also about having the confidence and knowledge to manage your finances effectively. In this chapter, we'll explore some tips and techniques for building confidence in financial matters and achieving financial success.

– Understand your current financial situation

The first step in building financial confidence is to understand your current financial situation. This means taking stock of your income, expenses, debts, and assets. Create a budget to track your income and expenses, and make a list of all your debts and assets. This will give you a clear picture of where you stand financially and help you identify areas for improvement.

– Educate yourself about financial matters

31: BUILDING CONFIDENCE IN FINANCIAL MATTERS: TIPS AND TECHNIQUES FOR FINANCIAL SUCCESS

Financial literacy is essential for building confidence in financial matters. The more you know about money, the better equipped you'll be to make informed decisions about your finances. Take the time to educate yourself about financial matters, including basic concepts like budgeting, saving, and investing. There are many resources available, including books, websites, and courses, that can help you improve your financial literacy.

– Set financial goals

Setting financial goals is an important part of building financial confidence. Identify what you want to achieve financially, whether it's paying off debt, saving for a down payment on a house, or building a retirement nest egg. Set specific, measurable goals and create a plan for achieving them. This will give you a sense of purpose and direction when it comes to your finances.

– Take control of your debt

Debt can be a major source of financial stress and anxiety. If you have debt, it's important to take control of it as soon as possible. Create a debt repayment plan and stick to it, focusing on paying off high-interest debts first. Consider consolidating your debts or negotiating with creditors to lower your interest rates or monthly payments.

– Build an emergency fund

Unexpected expenses can be a major source of financial stress. Building an emergency fund can help you feel more secure and confident in your finances. Aim to save at least three to six months' worth of living expenses in an easily accessible account.

– Invest for the future

Investing can be a great way to build wealth and achieve your financial goals. But it's important to invest wisely and understand the risks involved. Educate yourself about different types of investments, and consider working with a financial advisor to create an investment plan that aligns with your goals and risk tolerance.

– Track your progress

Finally, it's important to track your progress and celebrate your successes along the way. Regularly review your budget, debt repayment plan, and investment portfolio to see how you're doing. Celebrate your achievements, no matter how small, and use them as motivation to keep moving forward.

Building confidence in financial matters takes time and effort, but the rewards are well worth it. By understanding your current financial situation, educating yourself about financial matters, setting goals, taking control of your debt, building an emergency fund, investing for the future, and tracking your progress, you can achieve financial success and transform your life. Remember, confidence is key when it comes to managing your finances, and with the right mindset and strategies, you can unlock your inner potential and achieve financial freedom.

32: The Importance of Time Management in Building Confidence

Time management is an essential component of building confidence in all areas of your life. It is the process of organizing and planning how much time you spend on various activities to increase productivity, efficiency, and effectiveness. Proper time management can help you achieve your goals, reduce stress, and increase your sense of accomplishment, which in turn can boost your self-confidence. In this chapter, we'll explore the importance of time management in building confidence and offer some tips and techniques to help you manage your time effectively.

– Time management helps you prioritize your goals

Effective time management starts with setting priorities. When you know what your goals are and what's most important to you, you can allocate your time and resources accordingly. This means identifying your most important tasks and focusing on them first, rather than getting bogged down in less important or urgent tasks. By prioritizing your goals, you can work towards achieving them with purpose and intention, which can boost your confidence and sense of accomplishment.

32: THE IMPORTANCE OF TIME MANAGEMENT IN BUILDING CONFIDENCE

– Time management reduces stress and anxiety

Poor time management can lead to stress and anxiety, which can affect your mental and physical health, as well as your confidence. When you feel overwhelmed and disorganized, it's easy to lose confidence in your ability to get things done. By managing your time effectively, you can reduce stress and anxiety by staying on top of your tasks and deadlines. This can help you feel more in control and confident in your abilities to manage your responsibilities.

– Time management helps you stay focused and productive

Another key benefit of time management is that it helps you stay focused and productive. When you have a clear plan and schedule for your day, you can avoid distractions and stay on task. This can help you accomplish more in less time, which can boost your sense of productivity and accomplishment. Additionally, being productive can also improve your mood and sense of well-being, which can contribute to your overall confidence.

– Time management allows for work-life balance

32: THE IMPORTANCE OF TIME MANAGEMENT IN BUILDING CONFIDENCE

Achieving a healthy work-life balance is essential for building confidence and overall well-being. Effective time management can help you balance your professional and personal responsibilities, ensuring that you have time for both work and leisure. This can help you avoid burnout and maintain a sense of balance in your life, which can increase your overall sense of confidence and satisfaction.

– Time management helps you develop self-discipline

Effective time management requires self-discipline and commitment. By sticking to a schedule and prioritizing your goals, you can develop the self-discipline necessary to achieve your objectives. This can help you build a sense of confidence in your ability to stick to your commitments and follow through on your goals, both of which are essential for building confidence in all areas of your life.

– Time management fosters creativity and innovation

Effective time management can also foster creativity and innovation. When you have the time and space to focus on your most important tasks, you can also give yourself the freedom to explore new ideas and approaches. This can help you develop innovative solutions to problems, which can boost your sense of creativity and confidence in your ability to think outside the box.

In conclusion, time management is a crucial component of building confidence in all areas of your life. By setting priorities, reducing stress and anxiety, staying focused and productive, achieving work-life balance, developing self-discipline, and fostering creativity and innovation, you can manage your time effectively and boost your overall confidence. To improve your time management skills, start by setting clear goals, creating a schedule that works for you, and tracking your progress regularly. With practice and commitment, you can develop the time management skills necessary to achieve your goals and unlock your full potential.

33: The Role of Self-Compassion in Building Confidence

Self-compassion is the act of treating yourself with the same kindness, concern, and understanding that you would offer to a close friend in times of need. It is an essential component of building confidence, as it helps you to cultivate a positive relationship with yourself, accept your flaws and mistakes, and learn from them. In this chapter, we'll explore the role of self-compassion in building confidence and provide practical tips for incorporating self-compassion into your daily life.

– Self-compassion promotes self-acceptance

One of the key benefits of self-compassion is that it promotes self-acceptance. When you treat yourself with kindness and understanding, you're less likely to judge or criticize yourself harshly. This can help you to accept yourself for who you are, flaws and all, which is essential for building confidence. By accepting yourself, you can start to feel more comfortable in your own skin, which can help you to approach new challenges with greater ease and confidence.

– Self-compassion reduces negative self-talk

33: THE ROLE OF SELF-COMPASSION IN BUILDING CONFIDENCE

Negative self-talk is a common obstacle to building confidence. When you're constantly berating yourself for your mistakes or shortcomings, it's hard to feel good about yourself or your abilities. Self-compassion can help to reduce negative self-talk by encouraging you to be kinder and more understanding towards yourself. When you practice self-compassion, you're less likely to engage in negative self-talk, which can help to boost your confidence and self-esteem.

– Self-compassion fosters resilience

Building confidence requires resilience, the ability to bounce back from setbacks and failures. Self-compassion can help to foster resilience by teaching you to be more forgiving of yourself when you make mistakes. When you practice self-compassion, you're more likely to see failures as opportunities for growth and learning, rather than as a reflection of your worth or abilities. This can help you to approach challenges with greater resilience and confidence.

– Self-compassion improves mental health

Mental health is a critical component of building confidence. When you're struggling with depression, anxiety, or other mental health issues, it's hard to feel good about yourself or your abilities. Self-compassion can help to improve your mental health by reducing stress, anxiety, and negative emotions. When you treat yourself with kindness and understanding, you're more likely to feel positive emotions like happiness and contentment, which can help to boost your confidence and overall well-being.

– Self-compassion promotes self-care

Self-care is an essential component of building confidence. When you prioritize your physical, emotional, and mental health, you're better able to tackle new challenges and achieve your goals. Self-compassion can help to promote self-care by encouraging you to take care of yourself, both physically and emotionally. When you treat yourself with kindness and understanding, you're more likely to make healthy choices and prioritize your well-being.

– Self-compassion promotes positive relationships

Positive relationships are essential for building confidence. When you surround yourself with supportive, caring people, you're more likely to feel good about yourself and your abilities. Self-compassion can help to promote positive relationships by encouraging you to treat others with kindness and understanding, as well as yourself. When you practice self-compassion, you're more likely to attract positive, supportive people into your life, which can help to boost your confidence and self-esteem.

In conclusion, self-compassion is a critical component of building confidence. By promoting self-acceptance, reducing negative self-talk, fostering resilience, improving mental health, promoting self-care, and promoting positive relationships, self-compassion can help you to cultivate a positive relationship with yourself and unlock your full potential. To incorporate self-compassion into your daily life, start by practicing self-kindness, treating yourself as you would treat a close friend, and reframing negative self-talk into positive, compassionate self-talk. You can also practice mindfulness, which involves being present in the moment and observing your thoughts and feelings without judgment. This can help you to become more aware of your self-talk and to challenge negative thoughts with self-compassion.

Additionally, you can cultivate self-compassion by practicing self-care, such as getting enough sleep, eating well, and engaging in regular exercise. Taking care of your physical and emotional well-being can help you to feel better about yourself and your abilities, which can boost your confidence and self-esteem.

It's also important to be patient and gentle with yourself as you work on building self-compassion. It's not always easy to change negative self-talk or to accept yourself for who you are, but with time and practice, it's possible. Remember that self-compassion is a journey, and every step you take towards being kinder and more understanding towards yourself is a step towards building confidence and achieving your goals.

Finally, seeking support from a therapist or counselor can also be helpful in building self-compassion and confidence. They can provide you with tools and techniques for cultivating self-compassion and help you to work through any underlying issues or beliefs that may be holding you back.

In conclusion, self-compassion is an essential component of building confidence. By promoting self-acceptance, reducing negative self-talk, fostering resilience, improving mental health, promoting self-care, and promoting positive relationships, self-compassion can help you to cultivate a positive relationship with yourself and unlock your full potential. Incorporating self-compassion into your daily life requires practice, patience, and self-care, but the rewards are well worth it. With self-compassion, you can build unshakable confidence and overcome limiting beliefs, allowing you to achieve your goals and live the life you truly deserve.

34: Overcoming Burnout: Tips and Techniques for Building Resilience and Confidence

In today's fast-paced world, it's easy to become overwhelmed and burnt out. Whether you're juggling a demanding job, caring for a family, or dealing with personal challenges, burnout can take a toll on your mental and physical health, as well as your confidence and self-esteem. However, with the right tools and techniques, it's possible to overcome burnout and build resilience and confidence in all areas of your life.

One of the first steps in overcoming burnout is recognizing the signs and symptoms. Burnout can manifest as physical and emotional exhaustion, cynicism, and decreased productivity and effectiveness. If you're feeling overwhelmed, irritable, or unmotivated, it's important to take a step back and assess your situation. Acknowledging your feelings and taking action to address them can help you to prevent burnout from becoming a long-term problem.

One effective way to overcome burnout is to practice self-care. This means taking time to prioritize your physical and emotional well-being. This might include getting enough sleep, eating well, engaging in regular exercise, and pursuing hobbies and interests that bring you joy and fulfillment. It's also important to set boundaries and learn to say no when necessary. Prioritizing your needs and taking care of yourself can help you to recharge and build resilience in the face of stress and challenges.

Another important aspect of overcoming burnout is developing a strong support network. This might include family, friends, colleagues, or a professional therapist or counselor. Talking about your feelings and experiences with others can help you to gain perspective, feel heard and understood, and access valuable resources and support.

It's also important to cultivate a positive mindset and practice resilience-building techniques. This might include reframing negative thoughts into positive ones, setting realistic goals and expectations, practicing mindfulness and meditation, and developing problem-solving skills. Building resilience can help you to bounce back from setbacks and challenges and build confidence in your abilities to overcome obstacles.

Additionally, it's important to take steps to create a healthy work-life balance. This might involve setting boundaries between your work and personal life, delegating tasks, and learning to prioritize your time effectively. By creating a balance between your personal and professional responsibilities, you can reduce stress and prevent burnout from taking over your life.

In conclusion, overcoming burnout is essential for building resilience and confidence in all areas of your life. By recognizing the signs and symptoms of burnout, practicing self-care, building a support network, cultivating a positive mindset, and creating a healthy work-life balance, you can overcome burnout and build the resilience and confidence necessary to achieve your goals and live your best life. It's not always easy to make these changes, but with time, patience, and commitment, you can overcome burnout and achieve greater success and fulfillment in all areas of your life.

35: Building Confidence in Personal Growth and Development

Personal growth and development are important aspects of building confidence and achieving success in all areas of your life. When you focus on improving yourself and expanding your skills and knowledge, you can enhance your self-esteem, increase your resilience, and unlock your full potential. In this chapter, we will explore some of the key strategies and techniques for building confidence in personal growth and development.

One of the first steps in building confidence in personal growth and development is to identify your strengths and weaknesses. This involves taking a realistic and honest assessment of your skills, talents, and areas for improvement. By understanding your strengths and weaknesses, you can focus on developing your strengths and overcoming your weaknesses.

Another important aspect of building confidence in personal growth and development is to set clear and achievable goals. This means identifying what you want to accomplish, breaking down your goals into smaller, manageable steps, and tracking your progress along the way. By setting goals and working towards them, you can build momentum, gain a sense of accomplishment, and boost your self-confidence.

It's also important to invest in your personal and professional development. This might include taking courses, attending workshops or conferences, reading books, or seeking out a mentor or coach. By continuously learning and growing, you can enhance your skills, expand your knowledge, and become more confident in your abilities.

Developing a growth mindset is another key strategy for building confidence in personal growth and development. This means embracing challenges and setbacks as opportunities for growth and learning, rather than as obstacles or failures. By adopting a growth mindset, you can become more resilient, develop a greater sense of self-awareness, and build confidence in your ability to overcome obstacles and achieve your goals.

Building a strong support network is also essential for building confidence in personal growth and development. This might include family, friends, colleagues, or a professional mentor or coach. By surrounding yourself with supportive and encouraging people, you can gain valuable feedback and guidance, as well as access to new opportunities and resources.

Finally, it's important to practice self-care and prioritize your physical and emotional well-being. This might include getting enough sleep, eating well, exercising regularly, and engaging in activities that bring you joy and fulfillment. By taking care of yourself, you can reduce stress, improve your mood, and build resilience in the face of challenges and setbacks.

In conclusion, building confidence in personal growth and development is essential for achieving success and fulfillment in all areas of your life. By identifying your strengths and weaknesses, setting clear and achievable goals, investing in your personal and professional development, adopting a growth mindset, building a support network, and practicing self-care, you can unlock your full potential and build unshakable confidence in your abilities. Remember, personal growth and development is a journey, not a destination, and with patience, persistence, and commitment, you can achieve your goals and live your best life.

36: Conclusion: Unlock Your Inner Potential and Transform Your Life with Confidence

Congratulations, you have made it to the conclusion of "Confidence: Unlock Your Inner Potential and Transform Your Life with Proven Strategies and Expert Insights"! Throughout this book, we have explored a variety of strategies and techniques for building unshakeable confidence and overcoming limiting beliefs in all areas of your life, from career to relationships and beyond.

We started by examining the importance of understanding your self-worth and how to cultivate a positive self-image. We then delved into the power of positive self-talk, building resilience, managing time effectively, and practicing self-compassion. We explored how to overcome burnout, build confidence in financial matters, and build confidence in personal growth and development.

It is important to note that building confidence is not a one-time event, but rather a journey that requires dedication, perseverance, and continuous effort. With this in mind, it is important to remember that setbacks and failures are a natural part of the process, and that it is possible to learn and grow from these experiences.

As you continue on your journey to building unshakeable confidence, it is important to remain committed to your goals and to practice the strategies and techniques outlined in this book. Remember that building confidence is a process that takes time, effort, and patience, but the rewards are worth it.

By building confidence, you can unlock your inner potential and transform your life in countless ways. You can achieve your goals, build meaningful relationships, pursue your passions, and live a life that is fulfilling and rewarding.

In conclusion, building confidence is a lifelong journey that requires dedication, perseverance, and a willingness to take risks and learn from mistakes. With the strategies and techniques outlined in this book, you can build unshakeable confidence and overcome limiting beliefs in all areas of your life. So go forth, unlock your inner potential, and transform your life with confidence!

Thank You

As we reach the end of this book, I want to say thanks for reading this book.

I want to get this information out to as many people as possible. If you found this book helpful, I would greatly appreciate you leaving me a review. This helps others find the book as well.

Disclaimer

This document is geared towards providing exact and reliable information in regards to the topic and issue covered. The publication is sold on the idea that the publisher is not required to render an accounting, officially permitted, or otherwise, qualified services. If advice is necessary, legal, financial, medical or professional, a practiced individual in the profession should be ordered.

This information is not presented by a financial or medical practitioner and is for entertainment, educational and informational purposes only. The content is not intended as a substitute for professional medical advice, diagnosis, or treatment. Always seek the advice of your physician or other qualified health care provider with any questions you may have regarding a medical condition. Never disregard professional medical advice or delay in seeking it because of something you have read.

The information provided herein is stated to be truthful and consistent, in that any liability, in terms of inattention or otherwise, by any usage or abuse of any policies, processes, or directions contained within is the solitary and utter responsibility of the recipient reader. Under no circumstances

DISCLAIMER

will any legal responsibility or blame be held against the publisher for any reparation, damages, or monetary loss due to the information herein, either directly or indirectly.

www.ingramcontent.com/pod-product-compliance
Lightning Source LLC
Chambersburg PA
CBHW060536130626
46553CB00002B/783